D0443272

The Quotable

Oscar

Wilde

Library of Congress Cataloging-in-Publication Number 00-131311

ISBN 978-0-7624-0573-2

This book may be ordered by mail from the publisher.
Please include $1.00 for postage and handling.
But try your bookstore first!

Running Press Book Publishers
2300 Chestnut Street
Philadelphia, PA 19103-4371·

Visit us on the web!
www.runningpress.com

THE QUOTABLE

OSCAR
WILDE

by Sheridan Morley

RUNNING PRESS
PHILADELPHIA • LONDON

Contents

Introduction

*G*iven that this celebration of the Wilde wit marks the centenary of his death in Paris in 1900 ("it's the wallpaper or me, one of us has to go"), it may seem a little curious for me to claim that I owe Oscar my life; but that is the literal truth. In the late 1930s, my father Robert Morley was the first actor to play Wilde on the London stage, and thirty years later he was also the first actor to play him on film. But it was the initial run of *Oscar Wilde* on Broadway that first established my father's stardom. Opposite him in the original cast (as Lord Alfred

Douglas) was a young English actor called John Buckmaster, the son of Gladys Cooper, and like his mother intent on a stage career.

By the time the Broadway run of the play ended, it was clear that there was to be a war in Europe. Buckmaster decided that rather than return home, he would stay in the United States and, if necessary, fight with the Canadian rather than the British army. He did however have a sister Joan, still in London, and asked my father if he would carry some presents home to her. My father duly returned to England, looked up

Buckmaster's sister, took her the gifts, and subsequently married her. I was born a couple of years after that.

So Oscar has always been kind of central to my life. Although I cannot claim to be a Wilde scholar, I was once asked to write his biography. I was just about to decline, when by chance a publisher showed me a remarkable cache of photographs taken at the Paris Exhibition of 1900. Until then, conventional wisdom had it that Oscar spent the last few months of his life in deep Parisian penury before dying of neglect; but there in these photographs, taken six months before his death, is a wonderfully dressed Wilde with a showgirl on each arm and a heavy gold watch-chain, proudly posing beneath the brand new Eiffel Tower. So although his actual death was clearly lonely and agonizing, it is good to know that a few months earlier the good old Oscar was still very much in evidence.

The story of his decline and fall is too familiar to need retelling here; but in collecting just a few of his thousands of epigrams, it occurs to me that the master playwright lived and died just a bit too early. Not only would he have made a brilliant television talk show host, but the speed and variety of his wit would have guaranteed him a column in any periodical in the world. He died at the very start of the century in which he would have been so much happier, better understood, and so much more gainfully employed. If Oscar Wilde was a martyr to anything, it was surely to the kind of bad timing he would never have allowed in any of his plays.

Sheridan Morley

OSCAR

ON WOMEN
(AND MEN)

Women are sphinxes without secrets.

American women
are pretty and charming:
little oases of elegant
unreasonableness in a vast
desert of practical
common sense.

❧

MANY AMERICAN WOMEN,
ON LEAVING THEIR NATIVE
LAND, ADOPT THE APPEARANCE
OF CHRONIC ILL HEALTH,
UNDER THE MISAPPREHENSION
THAT ILLNESS IS A FORM
OF EUROPEAN REFINEMENT.

All women become
like their mothers,
that is their tragedy;
no man does,
that is his.

Never trust a woman
who tells you her real age:
a woman who tells you that
would tell you anything.

Women are meant to be loved,
not understood.

————⟩⟩————

A woman will flirt with anyone
in the world, so long as other
women are looking on.

WOMEN CAN DISCOVER
EVERYTHING EXCEPT
THE OBVIOUS.

If a woman wants
to hold a man, she has
merely to appeal to
the worst in him.

*Crying is
the refuge of plain
women and the ruin
of pretty ones.*

If you really want
to know what a woman means,
which is dangerous, always look
at her but never listen.

FOR FASCINATING WOMEN,
SEX IS A CHALLENGE;
FOR OTHERS, IT IS MERELY
A DEFENSE.

· 35 is a very attractive age:
London society is full of women
who have, of their own free
choice, remained 35 for years.

Women give to men
the very gold of their lives;
but they always want it back
in small change.

I like men who have a future,
and women who have a past.

MR. OSCAR WILDE.

If a man is a gentleman,
he knows quite enough, and
if he is not a gentleman,
whatever he knows is likely
to be bad for him.

Men become old,
they never
become good.

✢

THE WORLD WAS
MADE FOR MEN AND
NOT FOR WOMEN.

I sometimes think
that God, in creating man,
rather overestimated
His ability.

OSCAR

ON LOVE AND MARRIAGE

THE NIAGARA FALLS IS SIMPLY
A VAST AMOUNT OF WATER GOING
THE WRONG WAY OVER SOME
UNNECESSARY ROCKS; THE SIGHT
OF THAT WATERFALL MUST BE
ONE OF THE EARLIEST AND
KEENEST DISAPPOINTMENTS IN
AMERICAN MARRIED LIFE.

A man can be happy with any woman, so long as he does not love her.

The happiness of
a married man depends
on the people he has
not married.

The husbands of
very beautiful women
usually belong to the
criminal classes.

London is full of women
who trust their husbands;
one can always recognize
them because they look so
thoroughly happy.

*Twenty years of romance
makes a woman look like a ruin;
twenty years of marriage makes
her look like a public building.*

THE THREE WOMEN I HAVE
MOST ADMIRED ARE QUEEN
VICTORIA, SARAH BERNHARDT,
AND LILLIE LANGTRY. THE
FIRST HAD GREAT DIGNITY,
THE SECOND A LOVELY VOICE,
AND THE THIRD A PERFECT
FIGURE; I WOULD HAVE MARRIED
ANY OF THEM WITH THE
GREATEST PLEASURE.

The only real tragedy
in a woman's life is that her past
is always her lover,
and her future is invariably
her husband.

In married life
three is company,
two is none.

The proper basis
for a marriage is mutual
misunderstanding.

There is nothing in the world
like the devotion of a married woman;
it's a thing that no married
man knows anything about.

※

When a woman marries
again, it is because she
detested her first hus-
band; when a man marries
again, it is because he
adored his first wife.
Women try their luck, men
risk theirs.

I have always been
of the opinion that a man
about to get married should
know either everything
or nothing.

Men marry because
they are tired, women because
they are curious; both
are disappointed.

OSCAR

AT LARGE

OSCAR THE APOSTLE.
Puck's "Apple," Dream of an Aesthetic Plague for America.

Anyone can sympathize
with the sufferings of a friend:
it requires a very fine
nature to sympathize with
a friend's success.

A little sincerity is
a dangerous thing,
and a great deal of it is
absolutely fatal.

PERHAPS, AFTER ALL,
AMERICA HAS NEVER
BEEN DISCOVERED;
I PREFER TO THINK
THAT IT HAS MERELY
BEEN DETECTED.

OSCAR WILDE ON OUR CAST-IRON STOVES.

Another American Institution sat down on.

Of course America had often been discovered before Columbus, but it was always hushed up.

The youth of America is their oldest tradition; it has been going on now for three hundred years.

If you find a box labeled American Dry Goods, you can be reasonably sure it will contain nothing but their novels.

Education is a wonderful thing,
provided you always remember that nothing
worth knowing can ever be taught.

*It is a very
sad thing that
nowadays there is
so little useless
information
around.*

Ignorance is a rare,
exotic fruit; touch it, and
the bloom has gone.

The only duty
we owe history is
to rewrite it.

OSCAR WILDE AT WORK

By *Aubrey Beardsley*

Frontispiece

The English country gentleman
galloping after a fox—
the unspeakable in pursuit
of the inedible.

DEMOCRACY IS SIMPLY
THE BLUDGEONING
OF THE PEOPLE
FOR THE PEOPLE BY
THE PEOPLE.

*Work is
the curse of
the drinking
classes.*

I find that alcohol, taken in sufficient quantities,
produces all the effects of intoxication.

Consistency is the last refuge of the unimaginative.

A CYNIC IS A MAN
WHO KNOWS THE PRICE
OF EVERYTHING BUT
THE VALUE OF NOTHING.

Fashion is what one
wears oneself; what is
unfashionable is what
other people wear.

No great artist ever sees
things as they really are;
if he did, he would cease
to be an artist.

*Society often
forgives the criminal,
but it never forgives
the dreamer.*

There is no such thing
as a moral or immoral book:
books are well written
or badly written.

Examinations consist
of the foolish asking questions
the wise cannot answer.

Punctuality is the thief of time.

The truth is rarely pure and never simple.

OSCAR

ON LIFE

THE BOOK OF LIFE BEGINS
WITH A MAN AND A WOMAN
IN A GARDEN; IT ENDS
WITH REVELATIONS.

A HOUSE of POMEGRANATES BY OSCAR WILDE

THE DESIGN & DECORATION OF THIS
C. RICKETTS BOOK & BY CH. SHANNON

LONDON
JAMES R. OSGOOD
McILVAINE MDCCCXCI

The good end happily
and the bad unhappily;
that is what fiction
means.

We are all in the gutter,
but some of us are looking
at the stars.

Experience is the name
we all give to our mistakes.

The only thing worse
in the world than being
talked about is not being
talked about.

Children begin by loving
their parents. After a time,
they judge them; rarely if ever
do they forgive them.

The old believe everything;
the middle-aged suspect
everything; the young know
everything.

Nothing
succeeds like
excess.

IN THIS WORLD THERE ARE
ONLY TWO TRAGEDIES;
ONE IS NOT GETTING WHAT
ONE WANTS, THE OTHER
IS GETTING IT.

To lose one parent may
be regarded as a misfortune;
to lose both looks
like carelessness.

To get back one's youth,
one merely has to repeat
one's follies.

Young people nowadays
assume that money is everything,
and when they get older
they know it.

*It is better to
have a permanent
income than to be
fascinating.*

❧

NO MAN IS EVER
RICH ENOUGH TO BUY
BACK HIS PAST.

A man cannot be too careful in his choice of enemies.

Every great man
nowadays has his
disciples, but it is always
Judas who writes
the biography.

OSCAR

WHEN I HAD TO FILL
IN THE IMMIGRATION PAPERS,
I GAVE MY AGE AS 19, AND
MY PROFESSION AS GENIUS;
I ADDED THAT I HAD
NOTHING TO DECLARE
EXCEPT MY TALENT.

I have put my genius
into my life, whereas all
I have put into my work
is my talent.

I can resist everything except temptation.

I HAVE VERY
SIMPLE TASTES,
I AM ALWAYS
SATISFIED WITH
THE VERY BEST.

I like talking to a brick wall,
I find it is the only thing that
never contradicts me.

Whenever people
agree with me,
I always feel
I must be wrong.

One half of the world
does not believe in God,
and the other half
does not believe in me.

PRAISE MAKES ME HUMBLE,
BUT WHEN I AM ABUSED
I KNOW I HAVE TOUCHED
THE STARS.

I shall have to die,
as I have lived,
beyond my means.

To regain my youth
I would do anything
in the world, except take
exercise, get up early,
or become respectable.

If this is the way
Queen Victoria treats her
prisoners, she doesn't
deserve to have any.

I shall never make a new friend in life, though I rather hope to make a few in death.

I have had my hand on the moon;
what is the use of trying to rise
a little way from the ground?

OSCAR WILDE ON THE PLATFORM.

THE FAMOUS AESTHETE POSING AND "MASHING" ON HIS SHAPE AT CHICKERING HALL, NEW YORK CITY

This wallpaper will be
the death of me;
one of us will have to go.

photography credits:
Mary Evans Picture Library:
pages 30, 45, 48, 67, 75, 83, 107, 125
Popperfoto/Archive Photos: pages 35, 122
Library of Congress:
pages 13, 14, 20, 37, 38, 55, 59, 64, 85, 89,
90, 94, 101, 102, 112-113, 121, 126

This book has been bound using
handcraft methods and Smyth-sewn
to ensure durability.

The dust jacket and interior were
designed by Bryn Ashburn.

Photo research was executed
by Susan Oyama.

The text was edited by Marc Frey.

The text was set in Milton, Bodega, Engravers,
Poppl Residenz, Arnold Bocklin, Theatre
Antoine, Type Embellishments
One and Two.